GW00724492

PARACHUTING

AND

SKYDIVING

PARACHUTING AND SKYDIVING

Sally Smith

Pelham Books

Acknowledgements

Technical advice: Gordon Lilly
Photographs: Symbiosis (including front
cover), Charles Shea-Simonds, Terry
Crawley, Gary Mills, Andy Keech
(including back cover) and others
Sketches: Andy Wadhams

First published in Great Britain by
Pelham Books Ltd, 52 Bedford Square,
London WC1B 3EF   1978

ISBN 0 7207 1063 4

Printed in Great Britain by
BAS Printers Limited, Over Wallop, Hampshire
and bound by Dorstel Press, Harlow, Essex

Contents

Foreword

by John Meacock, Chairman
British Parachute Association

Books about sport parachuting are quite rare; books about sport parachuting by an expert woman parachutist, extremely rare. Not since 1964 has a book appeared on parachuting by a woman, and this is the first ever to be written by a British girl. Sally Smith's qualifications are impressive. A journalist, she has made over 1200 descents, and has represented Great Britain in World Parachuting Championships. She is an active sport parachutist and is almost certain to be selected to accompany the British Team to the next World Championships.

Sally's book gives you a completely up-to-date picture, helped with some first-class photographs, of the phenomenal sport of free-fall parachuting as it is today. Beginning with a general description, the book goes on to describe the basic ground-training programme, a programme that can take as little as six and a half hours and culminates with the most exciting of experiences—the first parachute descent. The reader is taken through the system of progress in use in this country, and all stages of freefall training are covered right through to competition standards.

Through this book the reader will find that the sport of contemporary freefall parachuting is a pursuit that is thrilling almost beyond description, yet, with commonsense and an adherence to the rules of the game, it carries far less risk than is popularly believed.

March, 1978

Chapter 1

WHAT'S IT ALL ABOUT?

Skydiving has not yet become a major spectator sport. Most people's experience of parachuting is limited to odd bits they have read in the papers, the occasional demonstration they may have seen at a county show or fête, or tales of military parachuting, when the element of sport is very small indeed! Yet in the last decade parachuting has developed into a major competitive and recreational sport and hobby for civilians all over the world, with enthusiasts giving as much time and effort to training and practice as participants in athletics and other top Olympic sports. Skydiving is certainly a modern game, often described as 'the space-age sport'. Its progress and popularity have been increasing at a phenomenal rate, and it is quite rapidly becoming an established part of the annual sporting calendar.

Every parachute descent can be divided into two very separate activities: work in freefall and work under the parachute.

Freefall Work

'Freefall' is the term applied to the first half of the parachute jump, after the jumper has left the aircraft but before he has pulled his ripcord and opened his parachute. It sounds terrifying – falling down through the air with no support, nothing under you at all – but it's not. You are a long way up above the earth, literally up in the skies.

(facing) *Most people's experience of parachuting is from watching displays at county shows and fêtes . . . but there is far more to sport parachuting than that.*

9

'Freefall' is the term applied to the first half of a parachute jump before the parachute is opened.

The horizon is miles away; the ground is so far below you can feel no imminent danger. And there is no sensation of falling at all. The air rushes past, but there is no real feeling of speed. You are floating up there in the sky. The view is amazing, the freedom is indescribable, and more than that – it is tremendous fun! But it is rare that a jumper just goes up and floats around in the sky enjoying himself. Usually there is work to be done.

In freefall the body can do everything an aeroplane can do except go back up! You can turn, do loops or barrel rolls, dive, or even fly across the sky, travelling over to other jumpers to link hands and fall together for a while. To be in full control up there in freefall demands balance, co-ordination, and more than anything – practice. So most jumps are working jumps, practising a manoeuvre, perfecting control and working towards a particular goal, perhaps a c or d certificate, or training for a competition.

Flying through the air is tremendous fun.

Under the Parachute

When you have pulled the ripcord and the parachute billows out above you, that's not the end of the jump by any means. You start on basic round parachutes and then you can progress to the modern high-performance canopies that are real flying machines. They can be turned and braked – even the descent rate can be increased or decreased – and properly handled you should achieve a tiptoe landing every time right on target. But it takes a lot of experience and a lot of practice in all weather conditions before you can even hope to achieve half this standard, and so, as in freefall, every jump is usually a working jump. Handling a parachute requires more mental than physical effort. Opening height and position, wind direction and speed, everything has to be taken carefully into consideration. But after a while, like driving, it all becomes a matter of

habit and you can, if you want to, spend a while enjoying the view, the silence and the beauty, before concentrating on your final approach and landing.

Well-known Myths

Parachuting is an exciting sport, but over the years I have met some people with very strange ideas about it. So here are some facts to straighten out any stories you may have heard.

1. One old favourite concerns the 'roman candle', but this is a left-over term from the Second World War when it referred to a streaming parachute that remained closed. The term does not exist in modern sport parachuting. Ask a jumper if he has ever had one, and he won't know what you are talking about!

2. Parachuting is today a very safe and controlled sport. Gone are the days of death-defying leaps and will-it/won't-it openings. The modern parachutes and their opening systems have gone through rigorous scientific development programmes and tests. Nothing is left to chance; hence the claim that parachuting is safer than football, cycling – even fishing!

3. Yes, you can breathe in freefall. Although you are going at speeds of around 190 km/h (120 mph), breathing here is no different from breathing on the ground – you are just not aware that you are doing it.

4. You are trained from the start to pack your own parachute. It is a very simple procedure, so that even students pack for themselves – under supervision, of course.

5. On your first few jumps your parachute is opened automatically from the aircraft. So that old question, 'What if I freeze?', doesn't apply.

6. Most sport parachutists use the term 'parachuting' to cover all aspects of the sport – freefall and flying under the parachute. Sky-diving is just another term for exactly the same thing.

(facing) *The square ram-air parachute is a real flying machine.*

Chapter 2
STARTING OFF

Physical Requirements

While few countries lay down specific physical requirements, you do need to be reasonably fit and possess good co-ordination and a quick mind. Minimum age limits vary a little from country to country. Generally you have to be sixteen to make a parachute jump, and there is no maximum age limit. Before you make your first jump, you will need to either sign a declaration or obtain a doctor's signed declaration to say that you are free from the following conditions: diabetes, epilepsy, fainting attacks or a history of psychiatric disorder. On top of that you need to be in good general health with normal eyesight (with or without glasses or contact lenses) and hearing.

The only thing that most people have to watch for is head colds. Normally parachutists won't even notice the changes in air pressure encountered in a high freefall jump, but if you have a heavy head cold you are advised to stay on the ground until it is better. Alertness on every jump is vital, so it makes sense that drink and drugs are banned completely before a jump.

As you progress into advanced accuracy work and other sections of the sport, fitness becomes more important, so that you can guard against strained or pulled muscles. Top competition jumpers often train with seven or eight jumps a day, and then you need to be pretty fit just to keep going.

(facing) *Men and women, tall and small—everyone can make a good parachutist as long as he or she is reasonably fit and alert.*

Where and When to Train

Most clubs run authorized training courses for students – and there are now parachuting clubs all over the country. They do vary a lot. Some are full-time centres with their own aeroplanes, dormitories, bar, canteen, and all the very latest in equipment and facilities. Others are little more than a week-end gathering of enthusiasts who hire a plane and operate from a small runway on an empty field – the 'bring your own thermos and tent' sort of operation!

But wherever you go, as long as the club is affiliated to the country's governing body of the sport (in the UK it is the British Parachute Association), you can be sure that your training will be thorough and your equipment totally reliable and safe. Stringent safeguards and training schedules are laid down and adhered to by every club, and so your choice of training centre can be made purely according to location and your need for accommodation and other extra facilities. The majority of clubs operate at week-ends only, but there are several full-time clubs now in business across the country. While it is possible to complete your training and make your first parachute jump in just one day, most courses are run over a two-day period.

Weather plays an important part in sport-parachuting, but there is no particular time of the year that is the best time to learn. Courses are run through summer and winter, and although it is obviously more pleasant to jump in warm sunny conditions, a parachute descent on an icy clear day in the midst of winter can be very exhilarating.

What to Take With You

When you start to jump all your equipment is provided for you, but many clubs ask student jumpers to bring a pair of firm boots, a one-piece overall or tracksuit and an ordinary crash-helmet with no peak or visor. While even these items can usually be provided by a club, it is a good idea to supply them yourself so that the fit is correct. There is nothing worse than spending a weekend in ill-fitting shoes and a too-tight overall. The boots should be rubber-soled and high enough to give ankle support, but they must not have outstanding metal lace hooks. The boiler-suit or tracksuit is for protection during the jump and on landing, and regulations insist that these are white or light-coloured so that every movement the student makes can easily be identified.

Chapter 3

THE FIRST TRAINING COURSE

The training schedule for first-time jumpers follows a well-established pattern (in the UK this is set down by the Safety and Training Committee of the British Parachute Association). A minimum ground training programme totalling thirteen hours is required, with at least six hours' training being given before the first jump. There is quite a lot to learn before you make your first descent, but it is not book-learning and usually it is all very enjoyable. Centres often supplement their training with a film and slides, and other jumping is usually taking place while the course is in progress, so that students can see all the theory being put into practice – which always helps!

Documentation and Routine Safety

There is a certain amount of documentation work that has to be completed before anyone can make a jump. Full membership of the British Parachute Association brings all sorts of benefits including a bi-monthly colour magazine and third-party insurance cover. Jumpers between the ages of sixteen and eighteen must obtain a written letter of consent from their parents or guardians, and everyone is required to sign a form of indemnity before he jumps. All jumpers are required to log every descent they make, and official log books can be bought at most clubs. But for beginners, the club usually takes care of all records for the first few descents.

All airfields are dangerous places for newcomers, and it is vital to be aware of the hazards as soon as you arrive at an active aero-

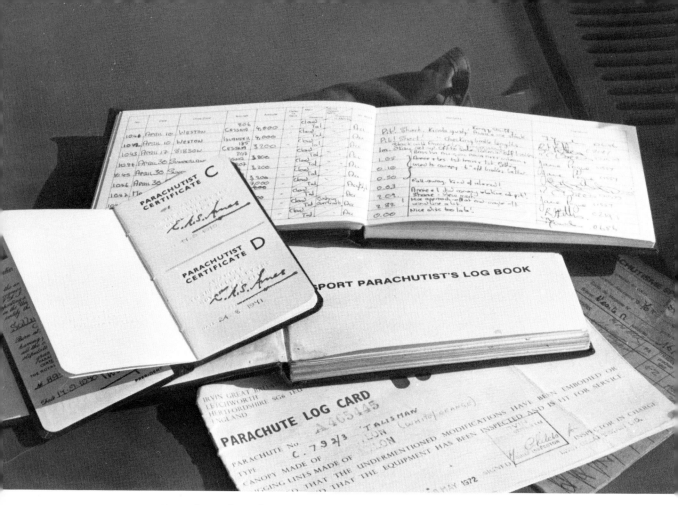

Every descent has to be recorded; your club will look after all the documents for your first few parachute jumps.

drome. Aeroplanes aren't like parked cars, and just because they are still doesn't mean they present no hazard. A pilot always checks there is no one around before he starts the propeller, but you could just be out of sight or not hear his call. So never stand near the propeller of an aeroplane.

At many parachute clubs, the walk back to the club house after a jump necessitates crossing a runway, and here there are definite regulations to adhere to. If the airfield has an active control tower, then the usual signal that it is safe to cross is a green flashing light. Always wait for the light, and then hurry straight across. If there is no control tower or the control tower is shut, then it is rather like road drill. Always look both ways, and check the ground for taxiing aircraft as well as the air for aircraft about to land, and listen too. Only cross when you are absolutely sure it is clear.

Don't ever smoke near the fuel tanks or the aircraft.

18

The Basic Parachute

The sport parachutist always wears two parachutes. Students wear a main parachute in a container on the back, and a smaller reserve parachute on the front. It doesn't take long to familiarize yourself with a parachute; they are not nearly as complicated as a non-jumper would imagine. The first few parachute jumps are usually made on a large circular canopy with a 'double-L' modification; 'modification' means the design or holes cut into the parachute to give it forward speed so that it can be steered. The double-L type of parachute has two L-shaped panels cut out of it at the back – hence its name. It is 8·5 m (28 ft) in diameter, and most are orange and white though nowadays other colours are becoming available.

Fig. 1 The 'double-L' type parachute has two L-shaped modifications cut in the back.

There are other types of student parachutes with slightly different modifications, but they are all very similar. When the parachute is open, the air rises up into it as you descend at a very slow speed. In the back the modifications let the air pass through, but in the front there are no holes. The air pushes on the solid material in the front of the parachute and rushes out of the holes at the back, giving it a thrust that forces it forwards through the air. It is this gentle forward speed that allows you to steer and land in the area you want.

The parachutist sits in a comfortable nylon webbing harness attached to the long lines of the parachute. The harness is attached to the lines by four long strips of wide nylon webbing known as risers. On two of the risers there is a small loop, through which passes

19

You soon get used to the equipment.

a line with a toggle on the end. These are the two steering lines, one on the right and one on the left of the jumper. It is a very simple matter to pull down on the right toggle to go right, and to pull down on the left toggle to go left. Hence you can turn the parachute to face any direction and move slowly wherever you want to go.

This main parachute and the lines are all contained in a small nylon pack that is worn on the back. It will seem a bit bulky and heavy to wear to begin with, but this is really due to unfamiliarity and after a few jumps it won't seem nearly so heavy.

So How Does the Parachute Open?

There are many systems in use now, but to start with let's look at the main methods used. Although we can't see or feel it, air is a fairly solid mass. When it is really windy, think of the force air has as it lifts dustbin lids, cardboard boxes and so on. When you are falling through the air, the air rushing up around you creates a similar force, and it is this force that opens the parachute.

The main deployment device used by freefall students is a sleeve system, when the parachute is folded and contained in a long fabric sleeve. Attached to the top of the sleeve by means of a length of nylon webbing, called a bridle line, is the pilot chute, which is a small parachute-shaped device on a wire spring. The sleeve itself is attached to the apex of the parachute by another length of nylon webbing called a sleeve-retaining line. Coming out from the other end of the sleeve are the long parachute lines that run down to the harness. These lines are stowed in rubber retaining bands in such a way that during the deployment sequence the canopy itself remains in the sleeve until all the lines have reached full stretch. The sleeve, with the stowed lines, is placed in an outer container, then the pilot chute is placed on top and the outer container is shut.

When the outer container is opened the pilot chute, with its heavy steel spring, pops out into the air rushing past your body. The air immediately fills this tiny parachute and continues to rush up into it creating drag as your body falls down away from it. This means it acts almost like an anchor in the sky, and as you continue to fall away it drags out the sleeve with the parachute in it. The lines quickly come out from their rubber stows and the parachute canopy itself is dragged out of the sleeve. The bottom of the parachute comes out first and immediately catches in the air rushing past. The air rushes up into the parachute, billows it out and in fractions of a second the fully open and deployed parachute is there above you.

The other deployment system uses a square fabric bag instead of the sleeve. The suspension lines are stowed in the same way as with the sleeve system, and the deployment sequence operates in a similar way.

The ripcord opening system
The outer container that you wear on your back has to be opened at

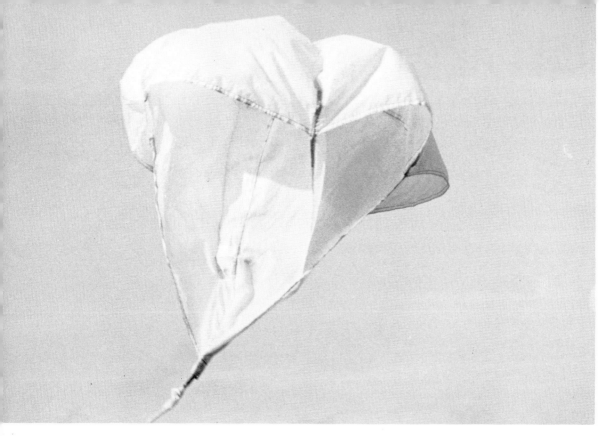

The pilot chute holds the air, creating drag as you fall away from it.

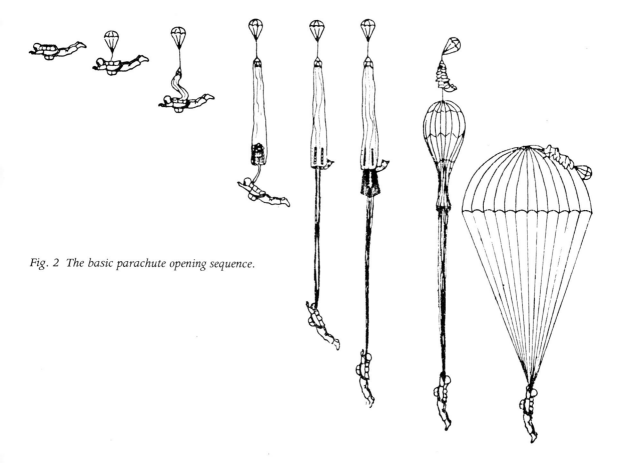

Fig. 2 The basic parachute opening sequence.

the right time to release the pilot chute which in turn pulls out the parachute. This means a way has to be found to keep the outer container shut until the right moment. The most common method still in use is the ripcord method. A ripcord is a long thin wire line. At one end there is a handle and at the other there are one, two, three or four pins sticking out, depending on the type of backpack being used. Back containers vary in design, but the opening principles are the same. The back container has four cross-over flaps, with eyelets on the edges of some of the flaps and metal or material loops on the edges of the other flaps. When you shut the container with the parachute and pilot chute inside, first the flaps with the loops are pulled across, followed by the flaps with the eyelets, so the holes fit over the loops. The pins from the end of the ripcord are put through the loops and the pack cannot open, however much the pilot chute underneath may be trying to spring up. The rest of the ripcord continues, through a protective metal covering called the housing, over your shoulder to the front of your harness, where the handle is stowed in an elastic pocket. This is an excellent system as the pack remains tightly closed with no risk of accidental opening until you want to open the parachute. Then you just pull the ripcord handle, which in turn pulls the ripcord and locking pins. Then there is nothing to hold the flaps together, and so the pilot chute springs straight out into the air.

A three-pin ripcord holds the pack shut.

The static-line system is used to shut the pack of a student.

The automatic opening system

Students in sport parachuting don't immediately have to pull their own ripcord, as this could cause problems. They may not find it easily, or they may be scared by the unfamiliarity and not pull at all. So in every country there are laws to ensure that every student starts his or her parachuting career with automatically opened parachutes. Though automatic openings may sound very grand, the basic opening sequence is the same. But instead of a ripcord and a pilot chute, a long line known as a static line is attached from a strong point in the aircraft to the bag or sleeve. As the student leaves the aeroplane, the static line is pulled taut and, like a pilot chute, pulls out the bag or sleeve and parachute. The end of the static line is tied to the parachute with nylon break tie. This is a specially designed nylon thread that breaks under a certain amount of pressure. It is strong enough to pull out the bag and parachute, but too weak to support the jumper under the parachute once it is open. So once the static line has pulled out the bag and the parachute has opened, then the tie breaks, leaving the parachutist free to descend slowly to the earth and the static line still attached to the aircraft.

Reserve Parachutes

Every parachutist always wears a second parachute in the very unlikely event of an emergency. Sometimes these are worn in a small extra container on the back, but students always wear them on the front, attached high up to their harness. Reserve parachutes are small round canopies with no or very basic modifications, and therefore very limited steering ability. They have been designed simply to open instantly and to let you down to earth gently and safely. They open in a similar way to the main parachute, but do not have a bag or any inside container at all. The lines are stowed in rubber bands fixed to the inside of the pack, with the parachute carefully folded in on top. The pack is shut with a small ripcord. With no inside container to slow down the opening procedure, the parachute opens instantly once the ripcord is removed and the chute catches the air.

Stability

Stability is a vital part of sport-parachuting, and refers to the control of the body in the air *in freefall*. Once the parachute is open you sit comfortably in a harness, so stability doesn't apply. But in freefall, after you have left the aircraft and before the parachute is opened, stability is vital. Once you have mastered control in the air, it is easy to forget how difficult it was to start with. But without careful training a student could totally lose control and end up spinning, tumbling and turning, which would not only be very uncomfortable but also dangerous because it could interfere with the opening procedure of the parachute.

The basic position adopted in the air is a face-down-to-earth position with the body in line with the earth and the arms and legs extended; the body is arched, so that the head, arms and legs are slightly raised. If you keep in this position, with arched back and arms and legs extended, it ensures that you will fall stably through the air. A good tip to help keep this arched position is to keep your head high. If you look up you automatically arch your back, and if you make sure your legs are stretched and your arms are out for balance, you should achieve the perfect student position. This means a student should *not* be looking at the ground until after the parachute is opened. If you tip your head to look down you may bend your shoulders down too, and quickly lose control in the air.

Practice on the ground

This basic stable spread position can easily be practised on the ground, and all students should spend some time achieving a good position so that it comes easily when they make their first parachute jump. Large centres will be equipped with suspended harnesses that will hold you up in the air while you practise the position. Other clubs will just lay out rubber mats or choose a clean area of soft grass for you to practise on. It is quite strenuous to begin with,

The basic stable spread position must be practised on the ground before the jump.

26

A small high-wing aeroplane is the most common type of aircraft used for parachuting. Note that the door and seats have been removed.

stretching out and back. Keeping your head up makes all the difference, and pointing the toes helps to keep the legs extended. After you have done a few jumps, you will find your own natural stable position that will be totally comfortable and require almost no effort at all. But to begin with everyone must start from the very arched and stretched spread position to ensure stability and hence a good clean opening of the parachute.

Aircraft Exits and Drills

You know a little about how a parachute works, and now you know a bit about how to fly through the air keeping stable and in control. Getting into the aircraft and leaving it correctly requires quite a bit of knowledge and practice too. Most students will be despatched for their early jumps from small high-wing aeroplanes. The passenger door of the aircraft will have been removed, and usually all the passenger seats are taken out as well. This leaves a nice clear area for the instructor and the students to work from. Every student will be despatched by a fully qualified instructor, and for safety and instructional reasons the instructor will always take the position nearest the door. Getting into the aircraft with the heavy parachute

27

With the seats removed, the parachutists can sit comfortably and move around safely with their equipment on.

on your back will seem very strange to begin with, and it is easy to be clumsy. So always climb into the aircraft slowly and very carefully, paying particular attention not to bang your pack on the door frame.

Exiting the plane for a jump

Once the plane has reached the required height – in the case of first-time jumpers it will be around 750 m (2500 ft) – the pilot will level the plane up and fly in a direction into wind over the airfield. The instructor will have already determined the correct exit point and will give last-minute instructions to the pilot to make sure the plane is in exactly the right position. Once the instructor is happy with the position of the plane, he will ask the pilot to 'cut'. By cut, he means to throttle back the aeroplane to as slow a speed as possible, to reduce the slipstream as you exit. He will then indicate that the time has come for you to leave.

28

You have to get your feet right to make a decent exit, and this is why practice on the ground is so important. On most high-wing aircraft used for students there is a special metal step fitted outside the door. You aim to end up standing cleanly on this step, facing towards the front of the aircraft and holding firmly onto the strut of the aircraft to avoid being blown off. It is from this calm standing position that you can step off backwards into a good arched stable position. In certain aircraft you will sit by the open door, legs dangling, and push yourself off with your hands. It is really quite straightforward, but whatever plane you use you must remember to keep a firm grip at all times and to make your movements definite and vigorous. The slipstream feels quite strong until you are used to it, and it can catch you unawares unless you are well prepared.

Different aircraft have different exit drills, and it is best to practise your exit several times on the ground, getting used to an instructor calling 'cut' and climbing out with the parachute and harness on and fully done up, so that you get some idea of moving around with the equipment on.

Once you have perfected getting out of the aircraft, the next thing to master is the technique of jumping off. Do this right, and you will fall automatically into the basic stable spread position. Once you have managed to get out onto the step, bent slightly forward, clutching the strut and standing steady (or in some aircraft sitting by the open door), the instructor will either shout 'go' or give you a sharp tap on the leg – whatever has been agreed on the ground beforehand. Then release from the aircraft in the way you have been practising on the ground. Whatever aircraft you are using, the important points are to be vigorous in releasing and to co-ordinate arms and legs so that you achieve the stable spread position immediately on leaving the aircraft.

Emergency Count

Parachuting is not a dangerous sport. However, everyone must know immediately what to do in the exceptional case of the main parachute not opening properly.

Once you have left the step of the aircraft, the static line takes under three seconds to fully deploy the main parachute. Therefore a student is taught to count this time, and if by then there is no fully deployed parachute above him he immediately activates his reserve parachute. The count is a very simple procedure. To count the proper time, you are taught to call out loud, 'One thousand; two thousand; three thousand; four thousand; check'. The thousand bit is only a delaying tactic so that it takes about a second for each number; by the time you have said four thousand, four seconds have passed. You start this count immediately you leave the aircraft. After counting and as you say 'check', you must always look up and check the parachute. In the most unlikely event of the parachute not fully opening, not flying properly, or if there is a tear in the bottom hem or a line right over the top of the parachute – in other words if there is anything that looks wrong – then you simply open your reserve parachute. This is very easy. You just pull the ripcord handle situated on the top of your front-mounted reserve, placing the other hand over the front of the reserve. Then you take both hands and throw the reserve parachute out and away from you. It opens instantly.

It is most unlikely that a student on a static-line-opened canopy will have no parachute above him. More likely, though still most unusual, is that the parachute will have somehow opened with one of its lines caught over the top, or some other disfiguration. By throwing the reserve parachute rather than just letting it open by itself, you will enable it to open instantly in the clear air away from the malfunctioning parachute above you. You will practise the emergency count and throwing a reserve on the ground several times. The count, of course, has to be remembered together with the stable arched position you want to adopt when leaving the plane – so there is a lot to remember!

Canopy Control and Wind Effect

It has already been mentioned that the modifications cut into the back and side of the main parachute make it fully steerable. In still air you will have a forward speed of perhaps 6 km/h (4 mph). The steering lines go up to the edges of the modifications in the parachute, and by pulling down on them you alter the shape of the modifications. By pulling down on the right toggle attached to the right steering-line, you distort and slightly close the right modification. This means some of the air that was passing through the hole before is now deflected and this decreases the forward push on this side of the parachute. But while you are pulling down on the right toggle, the left side of the parachute is flying normally with its full forward speed. So with the right side slowed down and the left side pushing

30

forward, the parachute rotates naturally to the right. Similarly, if you pull down on the left steering toggle you close up the left modification, and the parachute turns to the left. So the basic rules for steering a parachute are: pull the left toggle to turn left; pull the right toggle to turn right. You can turn a little bit or right round, depending on how long you depress the toggle, and by steering the canopy well you should have a good chance of landing right on target.

The wind plays a major part in parachuting, especially for students who use basic parachutes with minimal control. Whenever you arrive at an airfield or parachute club, it is a good idea to look at the windsocks and assess which way the wind is blowing, because this is the way you will be blown under your parachute.

At the start of a day's parachuting or after any definite wind change, an instructor or experienced parachutist will go up in the aeroplane and throw out a wind drift indicator (known as the WDI). The WDI is just a 6-m (20-ft) long piece of crêpe paper, 25 cm (10 ins) wide and brightly coloured so that it can easily be watched from both the plane and the ground. It will have a small weight at one end so that the total WDI weighs around 100 g ($3\frac{1}{2}$ oz). Its design has been very carefully calculated to simulate the drift of an unsteerable 8·5-m (28-ft) diameter parachute.

The WDI is thrown from the aircraft at 600 m (2000 ft) (the minimum opening height) right over the target, and is watched carefully as it drifts slowly to the ground. The idea is that it will show how far and in which direction a parachute will be blown that day. So if the WDI lands perhaps 100 m (300 ft) due south of the target, then the parachutist ought to leave the aeroplane 100 m (300 ft) due north of the target, so that he will be blown back onto the target area. This may sound rather a crude way to measure wind direction and speed, and of course today there are all sorts of technical equipment that can be used instead. But on the whole most people still choose to use a WDI to determine the wind conditions because it is so safe, reliable and cheap. If the wind is blowing from due north to due south, the area north of the target is known as being *up wind* of the target, and the area south of the target is known as *down wind*. So you will always exit the aeroplane *up wind*.

There are several basic rules to follow for good canopy control:

1. Use your parachute. This doesn't mean violent toggle movement, which should never be used, but it does mean control. Make up

your mind which way you need to go, then turn the canopy to face that direction. If you feel more corrections are needed, turn the canopy again. The parachute has been designed to be steered – so steer it!

2. Never pull down on both toggles at once as this won't do anything to help your steering.

3. If the wind is blowing, say, from the north, and your parachute is open due north of the target, do not drift too much to either side. If you go too much to the right the wind will still try to push you due south, and you will probably land to the right of the target. The same thing happens if you go too far to the left.

4. Once you are under your parachute it is not always a good idea to steer straight for the target, as you may find yourself directly over the target area at 300 m (1000 ft) or even higher. This means there is a lot of time left for the wind to blow your canopy further away before you land. So if in doubt, stay *up wind* and just ease your way slowly towards the target area. A good tip is to zigzag a little to the left and then to the right so that you are losing height up wind of the target.

5. A major rule is never turn the parachute near the ground. At about 60 m (200 ft) you must always turn the parachute into the direction of the wind to slow down your forward speed for landing.

Landings

While expert jumpers on high-performance parachutes gently touch down on tip-toe, students do land a little harder. The slightly faster, student landing rate is perfectly acceptable, but if ever a jumper comes back bruised it is because he or she has done something wrong.

The term PLF stands for parachute landing fall. The main impact from landing is on the soles of the feet, but to offset the impact the body then rolls onto its side and then back. This roll disperses the landing force throughout the whole body. But just like when you trip over or lose your balance, you tend to put out your hands to steady yourself, and this tendency has to be overcome so that you don't fall putting all your weight onto one arm, for instance, which could cause an injury. To land correctly, you need to keep your feet and knees tightly together, with the soles of your feet flat towards the ground, prepared for the landing. You need to bend your legs slightly at the knees, but still keep your legs directly beneath you – not up in front. You want to land on the soles of your feet, remember, not your backside! Keeping the legs together like this means the landing force will be absorbed by both legs equally. The elbows must now be tucked right in and a little in front of you – elbows are another hazard, and if you leave one pointing out and land on it it can be very painful. The final thing is to keep your head and chin well tucked down. Your head *must* be controlled, otherwise it can jerk back on landing, crashing into the ground. You must adopt this position a little above the ground in readiness for the landing.

At a minimum of 60 m (200 ft), turn the parachute to face directly into the wind. This means you are using your forward speed to push you into the wind. So if the wind is blowing at perhaps 12 km/h (8 mph), and you are pushing into it with a speed of around 6 km/h (4 mph), your landing speed will be 6 km/h (4 mph) going backwards. If you turned and steered in the same direction as the wind, a 12-km/h (8-mph) wind and your forward speed of 6 km/h (4 mph) would give you a landing speed of 18 km/h (12 mph) – a lot of difference. So an important rule is: *always land facing into wind*. Unless the wind is exactly 6 km/h (4 mph) or lighter, although you are facing into the wind you will be drifting slowly backwards. This is usual on most parachute descents. Also, you will probably drift gently to one side or the other.

When you land, first you take the impact on the soles of your feet and then you start to roll in whatever direction the parachute is drifting. After the feet, you roll onto the calf muscle on the side of the leg, then the thigh and the buttock, and finally you roll onto a rounded back. Your back must be rounded so that the roll can continue if necessary. Just before you land you must decide which would be the best way to roll – right or left. Sometimes, if you are facing directly into the wind, you will be drifting straight backwards, in which case you must turn your feet and body slightly to start a roll onto one side or the other.

PLFs are easy to practise on the ground. Most clubs start off with students practising on rubber mats, progressing to jumping backwards off a box or similar to try to simulate the landing. Some people find they can get them right immediately, while others constantly leave elbows out or forget to tuck their heads in. But keep thinking: feet and knees tightly together and slightly bent, soles flat to earth, arms up and elbows right in, head tucked well down. As you practise, try to feel the ground pass over your calf, thigh and buttocks

Parachute landing falls usually take time to master.

Fig. 3 A landing roll onto your left calf and thigh is known as a side left.

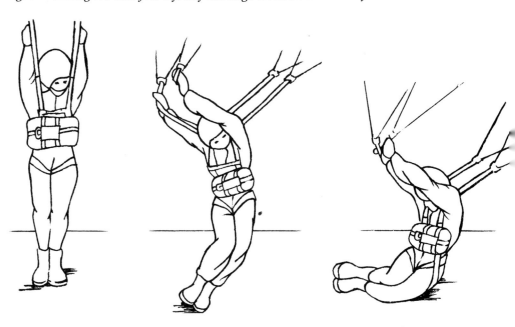

34

and onto your rounded back. A landing roll from your feet onto your right calf and thigh is known as a side right. A landing roll onto your left calf and thigh is known as a side left. You must practise both so that they come naturally before you make your first descent.

Some days, especially very early in the morning or late at night, there may be no wind at all, and you will find yourself drifting forwards in whichever way you point the canopy. Just because you are coming in forwards instead of backwards doesn't mean you have to use a new landing method. The basic PLF still holds good, but near the ground you must decide whether to take a side right or a side left landing, and then turn your body from the trunk down accordingly in preparation for the impact. You can still do the roll up the calf muscle, thigh and buttock and over onto a rounded back coming in forwards, but you must just turn the body a little to prepare for it. It is worth practising some forward landing rolls on the ground too, first on the grass or rubber mats and then jumping forward off a small box.

Obstacles

The name of the area where parachutists jump is known as the drop zone, commonly abbreviated to DZ. It is rare for a club to have a DZ completely free from hazards. Even on the clearest grass areas there is usually a tree or two, a few sheep, perhaps, or a low fence or ditch. Familiarize yourself with the drop zone you will be using before you take off in the aeroplane, so that you have some idea where the fences or other hazards are. Remember, your parachute will give a forward speed of perhaps 6 km/h (4 mph), so never steer yourself in the direction of a hazard.

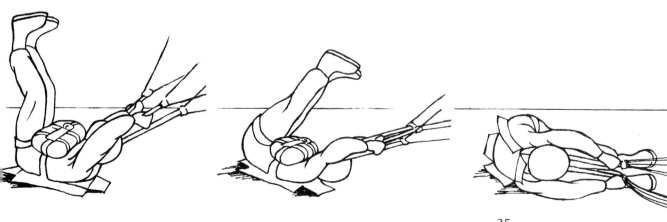

35

Chapter 4

YOUR VERY FIRST JUMP

Once you have been through the training you will feel a lot happier about your first parachute descent. The famous motto, 'Knowledge dispels fear', certainly applies in this sport, and by the time you make your first jump you will have a good idea of how the parachute works and what exactly is required of you.

You will have practised your PLFs, your stable position, your exit and count, and be well aware of the emergency drill. Your first descent may be made late in the evening at the end of your training or early the following morning. Sometimes weather clamps in or the wind gets up past the limit allowed for students, and you will have to hang around the club hoping and waiting. It is worth waiting for – you will never forget your first descent! Eventually your name will be called and you will be helped to kit up. The harness will be carefully fitted so that it holds you tight but is still reasonably comfortable. Your reserve will be fitted onto your front. You will have to wear a helmet, but goggles aren't necessary for early jumps unless you wear contact lenses or glasses. Gloves aren't necessary either unless it is very cold. Your equipment will be carefully checked and then you'll climb up into the plane. You will probably be instructed to kneel during the ascent. This means you can watch what is happening as well as having an easy position to shuffle forwards from when the time comes to exit.

It is easy to let the excitement of your first jump completely wipe all that careful training straight out of your mind. But don't let that happen. Remain calm and think carefully about what you have to do. Move forwards to the position by the door quickly but carefully as soon as you are instructed, then wait for the pilot to cut the plane and for the command to get out. Think carefully about your grip and the positioning of your feet. Don't be overawed by the fact that you are going to exit an aeroplane high above the earth. You as a jumper will be using the air as your medium, like swimmers use water. Concentrate on making a perfect first jump. When the command comes and you are told to get out, you will need more effort than you used in the practice sessions on the ground. The slipstream is quite strong, and you need to push your way out onto the step. Get out vigorously but carefully and position yourself comfortably on the step, holding firmly onto the strut and looking in at the instructor, waiting for the signal to go.

When it comes, don't let go in a panic. Remember your training, and *think as you go*. Jump back into a good arched position, really strain into it, and start your count out loud. Suddenly, in no time at all, you will be gently suspended under a large parachute. Look up immediately and check that it is in a full round configuration and all the lines are going up freely to the parachute. Find the control lines and take hold of each control toggle. Then look round for the target area and where you are meant to land. Turn the canopy, to find out how quickly it responds and to check how far down you need to pull each toggle to make the parachute turn. Have a quick look round by all means; you'll be surprised by the quietness and by how far you can see. Then check your drift, estimate your travelling speed and just try to judge it as best you can.

Suddenly, probably sooner than you expected, the ground will become very near. Make sure you have turned the canopy so that it is facing into the wind. Do this higher rather than lower – 60 m (200 ft) is about the right height – and check you are not drifting back onto any obstacle. Then get into your landing position – feet and knees well together, soles of the feet flat to earth, elbows in, head tucked well down. If you have got into this position too high, don't straighten out as you have a look, or you can be sure you will land at that moment! Just hold the position – although your head is tucked well down you can keep looking and get some idea of when you are about to land.

Suddenly you will be down – remember your roll, and keep your elbows and head well in. As soon as you have landed, get up quickly so everyone can see you are O.K. It is unlikely to be windy enough to keep the parachute inflated, but if by bad luck a small gust comes

You must try to keep a good arched position while your parachute opens. Look up at the aircraft, rather than down at the ground as this student is doing.

along as you land and starts to drag you along the ground, quickly pull down on one control line. This will spin the parachute into the earth, so that you can stand up and fully collapse it. Once down, you will have a tremendous sense of exhilaration and achievement. But save most of the chat until the parachute is safely back at the club house and put away. It is quite likely another student will be waiting to use the equipment you have on, and parachutes today are worth too much money to be left lying around for longer than necessary.

Chapter 5

PROGRESSING TO FREEFALL

To begin with, static-line jumps will seem more than enough for you to cope with. There is so much to remember that you'll be exhausted mentally as well as physically after a day's jumping. But after a few jumps, when you can exit the plane properly and stretch out into that stable arched position immediately, and when you have begun to get a feel of canopy handling, you will be ready to move on. Once you have performed a minimum of three absolutely stable static-line descents and have completed the thirteen hours' ground training programme, you qualify for Category 2 (see list of categories in Appendix B).

Dummy Ripcord Pulls

The next step is to practise pulling a ripcord handle yourself – something you will of course have to do when you eventually move on to freefall parachuting. This practice is done with a 'dummy' ripcord. A ripcord handle is put in the pocket of your harness, but no ripcord is attached to it. A static line is still attached to the parachute so that your pack will be opened automatically from the plane, just as in your previous jumps. This means you can practise pulling the handle out without actually pulling the ripcord.

In your early jumps you will already have noticed how easy it is to lose stability when you move an arm or a leg away from your basic arched position, and it needs a bit of practice and a sense of balance to be able to bring one arm right in to the body and to pull the ripcord handle without rolling over in the air. With both arms stretched out in your basic position you can feel really stable. It makes sense that if you bring in one arm the air pressure will push up the other arm and flip you over. So the answer is to bring the other arm in as well when you bring one arm in to pull your ripcord. But even that has to be done correctly. If you bring both arms in to your body you will have less pressure on the top half of your body, although the air will still be pushing on your legs. This will inevitably flip your legs up and you'll go into a fast steep dive – something you shouldn't be doing for a lot of jumps yet! So to be able to pull your ripcord handle and also maintain the basic stable position, you accentuate your arched back and hold your head high, and while you steadily bring your right hand in to the ripcord handle set in the harness on the right of your chest, you also bring in your left hand, bending your elbow at the same time, so that your hand is feeling the air just to the top and side of your head. In this way you can maintain your basic position while you look for the ripcord handle, grip it firmly, and pull it. You will probably be taught to go out in the normal arched position and keep that position as you start your count with *one thousand*. On the count of *two thousand*, look at the handle as you bring your arm in and begin to pull the handle out of its pocket. On *three thousand* you complete the pull and on *four thousand* you regain the stable spread. Then you check your parachute as usual. It is important to go back into the stable spread again once you have pulled the handle so that the parachute can open cleanly off your back.

You will need to practise this several times on the ground, kitted up in your harness and gear, to get the feel of bringing both arms in while keeping your back arched. It is very important to look at the handle before you take hold of it; otherwise you could grip the harness by mistake or lose a lot of time trying to feel for the handle. You will need to complete at least three consecutive good dummy ripcord jumps before you can progress to the next step – freefall.

Your First Freefall Jump

Your first freefall jump (when you pull the ripcord and open the parachute yourself) is probably almost as exciting as your first jump. For the first time you are going to be in control. You will have done several successful dummy ripcord jumps, and you should be beginning to get the feel of the air. Getting out of the aircraft will have

Your basic flying position in the air will begin to feel quite normal.

become easier, and your basic arched stable position will be feeling quite normal. It is natural to feel a little apprehensive before your first freefall, but it shouldn't worry you. You are only repeating exactly what you did on your previous few jumps – but this time your ripcord handle will be attached to the ripcord itself. The only possible difference is that you may need to pull the handle fractionally harder. And once you have pulled the handle out from the pocket you must continue to pull it firmly down and away from you, so that the ripcord itself comes right out. The ripcord runs forward from the backpack over your shoulder through a narrow metal housing to the front of your harness, and you must follow this direction in your pull so that the ripcord slides out easily without having to go round any sharp angles.

The instructor will still be spotting for you (that is, directing the aircraft and telling you when to exit), and you will still be getting out at between 750 m (2500 ft) and 850 m (2800 ft) above the drop zone. You will be concentrating intently on your first freefall, but do remember to make all your movements steadily. As before, *look* at the ripcord handle as you pull, and go straight back into a good arched position. It may take fractionally longer for your parachute to open under the ripcord system than with the static-line system, but really there is very little difference. Of course, you must still remember to count and to check your parachute – this must become a habit on every jump. If by the remotest chance you do have a problem on your early freefall jumps, then drop the ripcord immediately as you go in for your reserve ripcord. But as long as there are no problems it is a good idea to try to keep hold of the ripcord. They are expensive items, and once dropped from 600 m (2000 ft) they are almost impossible to find again. Most people slip them onto their wrists, leaving both hands free for steering. Other people pop them back into the elastic pocket on the harness; others tuck them between their body and the reserve pack. Do whatever is comfortable for you.

Once you feel you can pull your own ripcord without too much difficulty and have got used to the feel of it, you can concentrate a little more on your direction in freefall. Every time you leave the aircraft you should be facing the same direction as the aircraft is flying, and even when the parachute opens you should still be facing in that direction. As you come in for your pull, try to keep this heading. If you find you are turning to the right or left, it means your arms are not coming in equally or that your legs are not equal. Go back to the harness on the ground and practise your basic position so that you know you are doing it right.

(facing) *You must continue with your emergency count as your parachute opens.*

42

5-, 10- and 15-second Delays

Once you have demonstrated that you can do a good freefall jump, you can progress to spending longer in freefall before pulling the ripcord. This is how a parachutist works his way up the progression ladder. First you may do several 3-second delays before pulling the ripcord, then several 5-second. Some instructors will then put you onto 8-second delays; others may put you straight up onto 10-second delays. How do you time these delays? By continuing the initial count that you did on your first freefall jumps. On a 5-second delay, for example, as you exit the plane and go into your stable spread position, you count: *one thousand*; *two thousand*; *three thousand*. On *four thousand* you reach for the handle, and on *five thousand* you pull the ripcord.

You will practise the count on the ground with a stopwatch, and every jump will be carefully timed by the instructor in the aeroplane and also by an instructor on the ground. So you can be sure that everything you do will be seen and commented on. In fact after every jump you will receive what is known as a full debrief, when the instructor will go over every part of the jump with you.

At first, to wait five seconds before pulling the ripcord and opening the parachute will seem quite a long time, but it will only take a few jumps before it feels really comfortable and you begin to enjoy the sensation of being alone in the sky. Doing a 5-second delay will show up any errors in your basic stable position, and you may find you have a definite tendency to turn to the right or to the left. This means that something is out of alignment – your legs or arms not even, your body twisting a bit at the shoulders, your head cocked over to one side. Check your position in a harness on the ground and try to stay right on heading on every jump. Once you have performed a minimum of five 5-second delayed openings, remaining stable in the air and looking and pulling the ripcord properly, then you will progress to 8- or 10-second delays.

By this stage your canopy handling should be getting better. You will be using the parachute to steer you where you want to go, and you should be able to judge how far you will be drifting. Your landings too should be improving and you should be able to do a good PLF. One common problem experienced as jumpers reach longer delays is horizontal instability. The head will sink, then the feet will sink, then the head will sink again, so that the jumper is falling down to earth rather as a leaf does. This is commonly caused

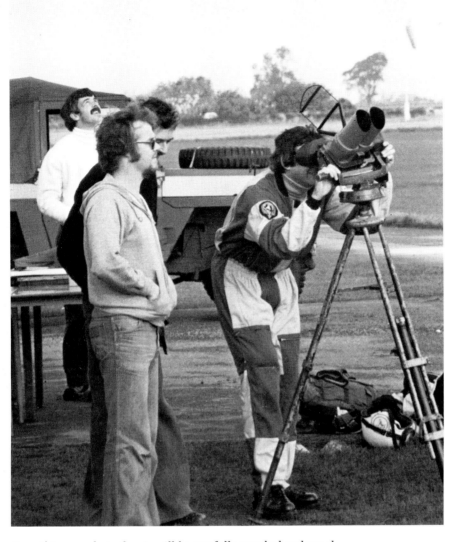

Everything you do in the air will be carefully watched and noted.

by having your arms too close together out in front of you. Widen your arms a little, still stretching out into the full arched position, and you will soon overcome this problem. You will find you can begin to adjust your heading (the way you are facing) more easily now. This is not only because you have had more experience but because there is more time in freefall to sort yourself out. You will still be counting your delays, and after a bit of practice on the ground against a stopwatch, to estimate ten seconds exactly should be no problem. Once you have done at least five good 10-second delays you will be able to progress to a 15-second delay, and this is quite a major step in a jumper's career, as for the first time you will be reaching *terminal velocity*.

45

Terminal Velocity

If you throw a stone off a cliff, you will notice that it gradually speeds up as it falls down to earth. It is the same with parachutists in freefall. After they leave the aeroplane, they gradually speed up. However, there is a maximum speed at which you can fall through the air. This is approximately 190 km/h (120 mph), and once you have reached this speed you will not go any faster. This is what is known as *terminal velocity*, or TV. And jumpers reach this speed 12 seconds after they have left the aeroplane. It may sound fast and frightening, but remember that a parachutist leaves the aircraft far above the earth and the parachute will be open by 600 m (2000 ft). Because the earth is so far away, the speed is in no way frightening. In fact you won't believe you are travelling so fast as there is nothing passing you to give an impression of speed.

On the first 15-second delay it will become obvious that you are leaving the aircraft much higher than before – you will be exiting from 1275 m (4200 ft). The climb up in the aircraft will take longer and the views will become more impressive. You must still do your stable exit and go straight into your basic arched position, counting throughout. As you reach terminal velocity, you may notice the air rushing past your face, but after a couple of jumps you will stop noticing even this. By the time you have done a couple of 15-second delays you will have done at least twenty jumps, and probably quite a lot more.

Students hit problems at different stages – some pass through all the early training and then have a problem at 15 seconds; others take ages to get onto freefall and then progress quickly. It is a very individual sport, and different progression rates are to be expected. But early problems don't in the least mean that you won't be any good, and if you look back in old parachuting magazines you will find that even some of the British champions have had very chequered beginnings!

(facing) *Once you are on 15-second delays, you should have no problem in leaving the aircraft in a good position.*

Instruments

When you are working on manoeuvres in freefall you cannot be expected to count as well, and as you go on to 20-, 30- and 40-second delays it becomes impossible to count this time accurately. So, once you reach 15-second delays you will be required to wear instruments, although you will still need to count to begin with.

The first instrument to get is an altimeter. This is a round clock-like instrument that tells you exactly what height you are above the DZ. You set it at zero before you take off, and on your jump as you descend the hand will pass slowly down from your exit height until it reaches 750 m (2500 ft). At this point you know it is time to pull your ripcord and open your parachute. The altimeter works on barometric pressure and is very reliable. But it must be set at zero before every jump. Different DZs will be at different heights above sea level and weather conditions can change the needle reading. So always check it is at zero before take-off. It takes a while to get used to reading an altimeter; this is why you need to count as well to begin with. But once you have got used to reading it you will find it easier to pull at the right height, and it will allow you to concentrate on the jump. But while you stop counting you must not forget to check the canopy on every jump.

The altimeter (left) shows height in thousands of feet; on the right is a stopwatch. Both instruments are fixed in a special panel attached to the top of a front-mounted reserve.

For a turn in freefall, you need only move your body above the waist.

Turns

By now your experience and confidence will have grown, and you will be able to fall in a more relaxed position. Turns are very straight-forward in freefall parachuting and can be initiated by dropping an arm, lowering a shoulder or even by raising a leg. To begin with it is best to start with quite gentle manoeuvres. To start a left turn, lower your left outstretched arm a little to the left and bring your right arm up a little to the left as well. Lower your left shoulder and raise your right shoulder from the waist up, and turn your head the way you want to go. Do nothing violently, and practise it on the ground first. You are only using your body above the waist; maintain your arch and keep your legs outstretched for balance throughout the manoeuvre. The first turn may not take at all, in which case emphasize each movement a little more. A 180° turn is when you turn 180°, ending up facing the opposite way. To stop a turn, just go back into your original position or even turn a little the other way. To go right, you do exactly the same thing but with the opposite limbs. Lower your right arm and shoulder, look the way you want to go, and you should go nicely round to the right.

Practise turns a lot until you can start them and stop them at will. Once you can do 180° turns your instructor will put you onto 360°, that is, turning right round until you are back where you started from. You will need to do quite a few jumps with 15-second delays and then 20-second delays, practising turns and getting used to the feel of flying.

49

Chapter 6

HAVING FUN IN THE AIR

Once you are happy using an altimeter and have learnt enough control to turn and stop in the air at will, you really will begin to understand the thrill of freefall parachuting. You will now be cleared to do jumps from 1500 m (5000 ft) with a 20-second delay before opening, and this greater height gives you longer to practise control in freefall. You may encounter your first cloud at this height. Parachutists never exit from a plane when there is cloud directly below, as this obscures the view and there is no way of telling whether you are getting out over the right point. But sometimes you will fly past little drifting clouds, and the first time you do this it will amaze you. As you float out there in the sky, suddenly a white wisp will tear past you at an incredible speed. It comes as a shock to begin with that it is *you* travelling at that speed and not the cloud!

Spotting the Aircraft

Once you are doing 20-second delays, you will begin to take more interest in what is going on inside the aircraft and the instructor will encourage you to try to 'spot' the aircraft yourself, i.e. direct the pilot to fly in the right direction over the chosen exit point. Good spotting is quite an art and can only be done well after lots of practice. Once the aircraft has reached the right height, the pilot will

(facing) *As you go higher, you will begin to understand the thrill of freefall parachuting.*

As you gain confidence, you can start to take more interest in what is going on inside the aircraft during the climb to height.

probably tell you he is 'running in' or flying directly into the wind. Remember, a WDI (wind drift indicator) is thrown out at the beginning of every day's jumping, and you will be shown where it has landed. You will have to assess how far away the WDI landed from the target and in which direction, and then work out a point directly upwind of the target and at the same distance. And that point is where you must direct the pilot to fly. If possible, try to select a group of trees, a large house, the corner of a funny-shaped field – something that is easily recognizable from the air. Pilots are usually asked to correct the plane with gentle flat turns, and usually only 5° one way or the other. So the usual call to the pilot is 'five right' or 'five left'.

It takes a while to get the feel of spotting. Also, as you approach the spot it is easy to ask the pilot to cut back the engines far too early. Never say the final 'cut' until you are at the chosen exit point.

Throwing a Wind Drift Indicator

You may get the chance to throw the WDI at the start of a day's jumping, and this again requires you to spot the aircraft. This time you need to throw the WDI right over the target, so you direct the pilot to fly the aircraft right across the target. When you throw the WDI, unravel a short length of the paper in your hand first, and throw it down through the slipstream with force so that it doesn't get blown back onto the tail of the plane. Once the WDI has left the air-craft, never take your eyes off it. It is very easy to lose, especially in the hazy heat of summer or on murky winter days. You must watch it all the way till it lands so that you can work out the exit point exactly.

Unstable Exits

While you are still on a 20-second delay, you will have to show your instructor that you really can control yourself in the air before he will let you go any higher. The idea is to show that you can get yourself back into a fully controlled stable spread from any position you find yourself in.

Instead of climbing out neatly onto the step, gripping the strut and leaping off backwards, the time has come to leave the aircraft in a more relaxed fashion. The nicest way to leave an aircraft is simply to dive out through the door, but unless you are prepared for it the slipstream can catch you unawares and flip you over as you dive. To counteract the push from the slipstream you need to dive out with your arms well forward and closer together than in your normal position, your body straight and your legs close together and bent up. If you keep your legs straight out behind you the slip-stream will catch them and flip you over onto your back. Some in-structors like the student to go out of the aircraft and bend forwards in a 'de-arched' position with his arms folded across his chest. This will put him into a fast unstable position. Usually he is asked to hold this position for three seconds and then flare out into his normal freefall position. If the jumper can quickly get back into a good stable position he will have proved he can recover control satis-factorily.

Tracking and Backloops

Once you have been introduced to spotting, mastered turns and practised unstable exits, you can go on up to 2100 m (7000 ft). This will give you half a minute in freefall before you need to open your parachute, and lots of time to play around in the air and try new things. But there are still several things to do before you can be passed out as a proficient parachutist.

'Tracking' is a word you will come across a lot. It is used on every jump where parachutists are doing 'relative work' – i.e. linking up together in the air and making formations. It is also used a lot in displays. The point of tracking is to be able to move *across* the sky as you speed earthwards. If you get it right you can travel right across the airfield, over several fields, or anywhere you fancy. It is a very useful thing to be able to do, especially if you have given yourself a bad spot.

To track properly you turn your body into a flying dart, hunched slightly forwards so that air gives you lift and speeds you forwards. This tracking position is quite a radical change from your normal stable position. You bring your arms right down to your sides, elbows bent and hands cupped forward to catch the air. Your legs should be closer together than normal and stretched out straight behind you, with your toes pointed. Your shoulders should be hunched round, but with your head up and pointing in the way you want to go. To begin with, go into this position slowly and steadily, and if you feel you are losing control flare back into your stable position and then try again. To move any distance you need to adopt a fairly radical position, and it doesn't take many jumps before you can do this easily. Don't forget to come back into your normal flying position after a few seconds and check your altimeter. You lose height more quickly in a good track position, and time goes more quickly when you are trying something new. Once you have got the hang of tracking, you can have great fun doing turns in a track position. You change heading just by turning your head and shoulders in the direction you want to go, but keeping your arms in and your legs straight. Always remember to open right out into a wide position before pulling your ripcord. This is known as flaring out. Never pull in a track position, as you will be travelling much faster than normal and the shock from the opening of the parachute could hurt. So remember to flare out before pulling.

Once you have mastered all this, the next thing to try is backloops.

Good jumpers can do backloops instantly and with perfect control, whenever they want to, but it takes a lot of practice. The main thing to begin with is to accept that you are going to do a backloop – that is, you are going to go right over backwards. Sometimes people start to do the loop and then unconsciously fight against it, which of course causes problems. To go over, bring your legs in by raising your knees as far up to your chest as they will go, keeping your lower legs and your feet well tucked in. As you pull your legs up, shoot your arms forward from their normal position so they are fractionally closer together and straight out in front of you, palms facing downwards to catch all the air. Push down with your hands as you bring up your legs, and throw your head back. If you do it correctly, you'll be surprised how quickly you'll flip right over!

The main thing is to bring those legs right in and up. If the air is still pressing on your legs you will have a real problem trying to complete a backloop. Watch out for the horizon appearing as you go over, so you know when to go back into your stable position. You will probably be able to feel when you are over, but watch as well so that you stop the manoeuvre at the right time. Try doing several backloops one after the other, so that you get the feel of them, and then do a turn and a backloop or a loop and then a turn.

You can start other manoeuvres now, too. A barrel roll is quite straightforward. From your basic position, bring one shoulder and arm in across your body and raise the opposite shoulder. Straighten your legs and put them together, and you should flip round.

Fig. 4 The backloop. By simultaneously bringing up your knees, throwing back your head and pushing down with your hands, you can perform a neat and fast backloop.

Forward loops are easy to initiate but they can be somewhat difficult to get right over. Bring your arms in and hunch your shoulders and bring your head right down, bending forwards from the waist. Keep your legs out in their original position. This should turn you neatly over. But try to bend your legs in once you are over the top of the loop, otherwise you could find yourself getting stuck on your back. You can actually fall stable on your back, but it is not advised as you can't see where you are going and also you have to turn onto your front to open the parachute. If you are on your back by accident, just do a neat half-barrel roll over onto your front again or put on a tremendous arch (which will also turn you back the right way).

Of all the many manoeuvres that are possible in the air, backloops, turns and tracking are the three that you'll need most for future jumping.

Introduction to Relative Work

Relative work is the art of joining up with another parachutist or group of parachutists in freefall. And it certainly is an art, for remember in freefall everyone is travelling at around 190 km/h (120 mph). Relative work has progressed so quickly in recent years that twenty, thirty, even forty jumpers now get together in the sky to form big stars and other patterns. But that needs a large aeroplane and lots of practice. So to begin with, a jumper goes out with an experienced relative worker just to learn the rudimentary skills required.

The first thing is to plan the jump carefully on the ground. In a simple relative jump one jumper will usually have agreed to go base. This means he will leave the aircraft first, and the rest of the jumpers will dive down and link up with him. It is very important that everyone leaves the plane as close together as possible. A time difference of only a couple of seconds between one jumper exiting and the next can mean a difference of several hundred feet between the jumpers once they are out of the plane.

Diving with your legs and body straight and your arms down your sides will soon get you down to any jumper below. But if you don't flare out back into your stable position soon enough you will find you have gone a long way below the other jumper, and then he will have to come on down to you. Once you are near the same level you need to move across the sky to reach the other jumper, and this can

Start your approach slightly higher than your partner, and move in slowly and carefully.

be done by straightening your back and legs and putting your arms out in front of you in a slightly 'de-arched' position. You may find you will lose height as you travel across the sky, so it is best to start your approach on the other jumper from a little bit above him. As you near him, slow down your forward speed by flaring out into your basic position again. If you have judged it right the forward speed you still have will take you gently in to the other parachutist, so that you can easily take hold of the excess material in his jumpsuit by the wrists.

Always remember that you are travelling very fast, so that if you misjudge your approach you can hit a jumper at quite a speed, damaging the equipment or hurting each other. A well-known tip for beginners is to aim just to the side of the person you are hoping to link with. This means that if your approach is too fast it is not danger-ous. If you are making a nice slow approach it is tempting to reach out to grab the other jumper too early. But a grab can send you sliding across the sky, so always wait until the other jumper is within really easy reach before taking hold of his jumpsuit. If you are leaving the plane first you must fall in a steady position, making sure you are facing one way and not turning. Also, while you can look up to see another jumper coming down to you, don't lift the front of your body up or you will slide back, which means the person coming in to link with you will keep chasing you as you slide further and further back.

The basic formation of relative work is a star, with everyone holding each other's wrists in a big circle facing inwards, and until you have quite a few relative jumps behind you this is the best formation to aim for. You will find that with three of you in a circle it may start spinning round. Just by altering your body or leg position slightly you can easily stop this. It is a good idea to tighten up your body position and tuck up your legs once you have linked. This means the star will fall through the sky faster and will be more stable. The further out your legs are, the more the star will tend to float and sway about.

When you are doing relative work time can go very fast, and it is essential that you keep a good eye on your altimeter. Well above the height at which you want to open your parachute, let go of the other jumpers, turn away and go into a good track for a few seconds. If the other jumpers do the same, then by the time you open your parachutes you should be far enough away from each other to avoid any parachute entanglements. Parachutes take up a lot of room and you can't afford to be close to another jumper at opening time. After you have linked and tracked away and just before pulling, make it a habit to wave both arms distinctly a couple of times. This should become a routine part of every relative jump. For just in case someone is tracking across above you, he will see you are about to pull and quickly clear the area. A wave-off is the standard signal to indicate that a jumper is about to open his parachute.

Before you are cleared to do unsupervised relative work you have to learn all these basics under the instruction of an experienced relative worker. Once you have qualified for an FAI C licence (details in Appendix C) you will be permitted to start jumping a high-performance parachute. These parachutes go faster, turn faster and can be braked – and come down more slowly, which means softer landings.

(facing) *A star is the basic formation in relative work.*

High-performance Round Parachutes

To begin with, you will probably progress to another round parachute, but with many more modifications cut into it. It is the impressive arrangement of modifications that gives the parachute its tremendous flying characteristics. One of the original and probably most famous of these parachutes is the American para-commander, commonly known as the PC, but today there are many other popular designs available, including the French Papillon and the Russian UT15. Jumping one of these high-performance parachutes is quite different from jumping the basic ones used by students. Openings should be more gentle and the controls will be much more responsive. The parachute will also fly and turn much faster.

An additional advantage is that you can brake this kind of parachute, something you couldn't do very effectively on a double-L parachute. To slow down the forward speed you pull down *on both control toggles together*. This effectively shuts the modifications at the back and reduces the forward speed of the parachute. The more you pull down on the brakes, the more radical the braking will be. If you pull down too far on the brakes, the canopy will lose all forward speed and go into what is known as a stall. In a stall the parachute stops flying and loses height very quickly, and it also becomes

With a high-performance parachute you'll have softer, more accurate landings.

The para-commander is probably the most famous of the high-performance round parachutes.

unstable. It is a good idea to find out how far you can safely brake the canopy and still keep it flying, but do this high up in the sky until you know the parachute well. Remember a tight turn or stall causes a rapid increase in your descent rate – something that should be avoided near the ground.

Because of the higher forward speed of the parachute you will find the spot is less critical, as you can make more headway against the wind and travel faster in the direction you want to go.

Cut-aways

Because of the high performance of these parachutes, in the unlikely event of their not opening properly they can become violently unstable. This means it is dangerous to open a reserve parachute while you are still attached to a malfunctioning high-performance round parachute. The main parachute will exert such unstable pressure that it is quite likely the reserve will not be able to open or fly properly. Therefore a new safety procedure is introduced when you begin to jump these parachutes. This is the cut-away method. If the main parachute malfunctions, you eject the parachute and let it go completely before opening your reserve parachute. This means the reserve opens in clear air with nothing to stop it flying properly.

Cutting away, as the method of release of the main parachute is called, is very easy, and consists of releasing the risers that attach the main parachute to your harness at shoulder height. There are several linkage systems in operation now that hold the risers and main parachute to your harness, with various methods of release. Usually it is merely a question of pulling down on a wire loop, a fabric tab or similar. As soon as you have released your main para-chute, you will find yourself back in freefall. Then it is simply a matter of pulling your reserve ripcord handle and opening your reserve parachute. You will have to practise cutting away several times on the ground before you begin to jump a high-performance parachute, and even after many jumps on it practise cut-aways on the ground occasionally. You may never need to cut away, but if you do you'll want to be able to do it instantly.

Ram-air (Square) Parachutes

Parachuting has advanced by leaps and bounds in the last few years, and perhaps the most exciting development has been the square

On a square parachute you should be able to land in the target area on every jump.

ram-air parachute. These are more like gliders than parachutes. In still air they have a forward speed of about 32 km/h (20 mph), which can be increased or decreased; they can be turned quickly; their descent rate can be increased or reduced. In other words they have tremendous control, and they are sought after by specialist accuracy jumpers and relative and style workers alike. Their unique control and wind penetration enables jumpers to land on or by the target on virtually every jump, and can make up for a not-too-good spot. But because of their high speed and critical control these parachutes have to be handled with care and are restricted to experienced jumpers only.

On your first few jumps no attempt should be made to land by the target. Instead, you should concentrate on slowing down the parachute's forward speed at the right height to ensure a soft landing. As with a round parachute, you brake the parachute by pulling down on both control lines, and the amount you pull down is directly related to the amount of brake you put on the parachute. The danger is in over-braking, when you can stop the canopy from flying, putting it into a stall and dropping you fast onto the ground, which may cause you very serious damage. So from the very first jump on a square parachute, some time should be spent at heights over 450 m (1500 ft) practising braking and going into the stall position. Soon after opening, at around 600 m (2000 ft), go into the stall by continuing to pull down the brakes until the parachute starts to waffle above you. Watch the parachute carefully and continue to pull down until it stops flying completely and drifts back behind you. Now experiment by letting up just a little on the brakes until the parachute comes forward and starts flying again. Usually only a little movement on the brakes is needed to get the parachute flying. Never stall the canopy and then let right up on the brakes, or the parachute will surge forward and dive in front of you. So on every jump practise this stall and stall recovery. The official instruction book supplied with new ram-air parachutes will mention the flared landing. This is done by letting the parachute fly at full speed for several seconds before landing, and then at perhaps 3 m (10 ft) or so above the ground pulling right down as far as you can on the control lines. This initiates a stall in the parachute, and if you judge it at the right height you can make a very gentle touch-down indeed. But you don't want to do this at the wrong height, so on your early jumps on a square parachute just brake gently to stop your forward speed as you come in to land, and only start flaring the canopy when you know a bit more what to expect.

A ram-air parachute can be steered easily to the left or right, but never attempt to make a sharp turn near the ground or you could hit the ground with force. As with high-performance round parachutes, the cut-away system is the only safe way to deal with an emergency situation. If you have an unusual opening and the parachute is not flying properly – get rid of it.

Chapter 7

DOING YOUR OWN THING

The real enjoyment in sport parachuting begins when you have done a hundred or more jumps. Then you have got over the difficult student stage and you can begin to have a bit of fun as you continue to progress. Leaving the plane will become as routine as hopping off a bus, and your mind will be free to concentrate on freefall techniques.

Accuracy Work

It is not only fun to achieve accuracy on every jump, but it is also pretty essential if you are going to continue safely in the sport. Once you have got the hang of controlling a parachute in the air and judging your drift, you can start to aim for the ultimate target. This is a small disc, the size of a beermat, that lies in the centre of the target landing area. At most drop zones there is a big round target landing area filled with shock-absorbing pea-gravel. This is called a 'pit', and the brightly coloured disc sits right in the middle. This is the point you are aiming for, and to begin with it can be quite frustrating to be sailing happily towards the disc and then end up landing way past it.

On round parachutes
The only way to achieve consistent accuracy is to forget all your early training about turning the parachute to face into the wind to land, and instead to come into the pit forwards. This means you are

facing the pit with the wind behind you. You can be travelling quite fast, as the forward speed of your parachute will be in addition to the speed of the wind. The idea of coming into the pit forwards is that you can make a steady approach right down the wind line towards the target, looking at the target all the way so that you don't lose sight of it for a moment. But of course you will need to use your brakes to slow the canopy down and keep it on the right line. Ideally you should fly the parachute with the control lines pulled halfway down, so that it is on half-brakes. Then if you find you are dropping short you can let up the brakes and get more forward speed to take you on into the pit. If, on the other hand, you are over-shooting the pit area, then you pull down further on the controls to stop the canopy a bit more. It takes a lot of practice, and it is best to start making downwind approaches in low winds until you have built up confidence in your accuracy approaches. When you have gained a lot of air experience you will probably want to transfer to the square ram-air parachutes. These are the ultimate accuracy parachutes, used by all top accuracy jumpers.

On ram-air parachutes
Watching a top accuracy jumper coming gently into the pit and stamping on the disc time after time makes it look all too easy! But in fact only a handful of jumpers ever reach this standard, and even then there is no guarantee that they won't make an error of judgment

(facing) *You need to be familiar with the braking characteristics of your parachute for good accuracy work.*

(right) *Top accuracy jumpers can make a tip-toe landing right on target.*

every so often. To achieve consistent accuracy takes a lot of experience, a lot of practice and a great deal of concentration on every jump.

On an accuracy jump you land facing into the wind just like on a normal jump. Because of the high forward speed of the square parachute, except in unusually high winds you will always have some forward speed. The wind line is important, and so that your final approach at the target is stable you should be facing directly into the wind. Once you have opened the parachute, you will have to lose quite a bit of height before you start turning in for your final approach. It is best to stay on the upwind side of the pit until you are down to perhaps 350 m (1200 ft) or less. If you go downwind of the pit too early it is easy to misjudge the strength of the wind and go too far downwind, only to find that you cannot get any forward speed against the wind to come back into the pit area. At around 350 m (1200 ft) you should still be on the upwind side of the pit but not too far away from it. Take a good look at the windsock to determine the ground wind speed and the direction, and then plan your final flight path and attack point.

Never fly directly across the top of the pit down the wind line, as you cannot turn a parachute round on its own axis. You can turn it pretty tightly by turning in deep brakes, but even so you will end up a little off to one side or the other. Ideally, fly down the side of the pit at around 200–300 m (700–1000 ft) on half-brakes. If you want to lose more height before making your final approach into the pit, go out to one side of the pit rather than beyond it. This means that if the wind suddenly gets up you won't be caught out downwind. Plan your flight path as you descend on the parachute, and turn in to set up, facing the target just a little way downwind of the pit. The distance you choose depends on the strength of the wind. In low wind you can afford to start your approach from beyond the edge of the pit and fly in to the disc at a steady glide angle. In a high wind you need to turn in over the edge of the pit as you won't have so much forward speed and your glide angle will be much steeper. As you gradually lose height, trim and brake the canopy to keep it facing directly into the wind, checking that you are on the right angle of descent to land smack on the disc. Even in low winds, never set up too far away from the pit. It is always better to be closer in and to sink the parachute down by using heavy brakes. This gives tighter control of the parachute and a steadier approach. A ram-air parachute flying at full speed is unstable and makes accuracy difficult.

You must keep your eye constantly on the target during your final approach.

One common complaint from accuracy jumpers on square parachutes is, 'I just couldn't stop the parachute', as they go sailing over and beyond the disc! So practise braking the parachute into the stall point and recovering on every jump at height until you really know your parachute. Good footwork is essential on accuracy jumps, as it is easy to work really hard until the last moment and then put the wrong foot down first or not make a clean stab at the disc with the nearest foot. It is the very first part of you to touch the ground that is measured, so make sure one foot is well out of the way as you go for the disc. By this stage you will probably have stopped wearing the

Toe strikes are probably the cleanest way of hitting the target disc.

heavy parachute boots recommended for students and will be jumping in light basketball or similar shoes. With these lighter-weight shoes it is easier to make a clean strike at the disc, and toe strikes are probably the cleanest.

Competition in Accuracy Work

Accuracy competitions are run either for individuals, when a jumper gets out on his or her own, or for teams, when perhaps three or four jumpers exit the plane together. There are many club, national and international contests every year. In individual events you merely have to worry about getting a good score for yourself. In team events you have to be continually watching your fellow team members and altering your rate of descent so that you don't get in each other's way when you are approaching the pit. Teams achieve good separation if the first jumper out of the plane delays for perhaps 8 seconds before opening his parachute, while the last jumper out pulls his ripcord immediately.

Judges will stand by the disc to mark your very first point of contact with the ground, and there will also be observing judges in case the winds go over competition limits or you have a control problem with your parachute, and to check many other details that are adhered to in strict competition. Electronic pads, with the disc in the middle, are now coming into use. These mark your landing point automatically and your score comes up instantly on a small electronic scoreboard just outside the pit area. This system is more foolproof than human judges, especially on fast approaches

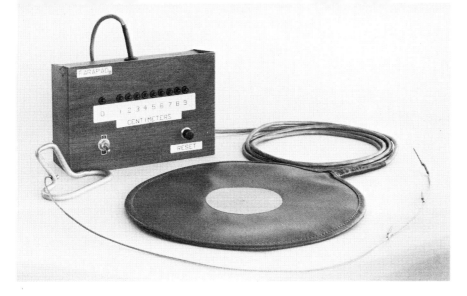

The new Parapad electronic scoring system, designed by American Jeffrey H. Steinkamp.

when the first point of contact is not always easy to pinpoint. Scores are marked in centimetres and metres from the edge of the target disc to a maximum of 10 m (30 ft), and competitions can have three, four or even ten rounds. Height for accuracy jumps is usually from 600–1000 m (2000–3200 ft) depending on whether it is an individual or team event.

Judges will mark your very first point of contact with the ground.

Style

The word 'style' doesn't instantly convey to a non-jumper what it means in parachuting. In fact it refers to a series of specific manoeuvres made in freefall. Style is the individual freefall event in competition, as opposed to relative, which is teamwork. A full style jump consists, in parachuting jargon, of a 'series' or 'set', and the basic movements for a series are two alternate 360° flat turns and a backloop, followed by two more turns and a backloop. It sounds quite easy on the ground, but to begin with it takes an amazing amount of concentration and mental effort to get through a whole series in one jump, and it is often best to start with half sets – just two turns and one backloop. The idea is to get the series really precise and fast, and once you have battled your way through a whole series in perhaps 14 seconds you will appreciate the skill and ability of the world's top style jumpers who turn a whole set in 6 seconds and less.

To turn good style you need to start from a very small basic position – that is, you make yourself as small as possible. This is quite a radical change from the relaxed stable spread. If you are falling in a small position, with your body bent and your arms and legs tightly in, there is less surface area to resist the air flow and you will fall faster. Also, it will be easier to make quick turns and loops. In a wide position you tend to fly around, whereas in a small position you can almost spin a turn instantly. Most style jumpers go for the small position with legs bent and tucked right up on their fronts and either arms down in front or with the elbows tucked well in and forearms sticking out to balance their bodies. You need to constantly balance this position, as it is very unstable.

To start with, just slowly work at this small position, getting in as tight as you possibly can. Bend your back and hunch your shoulders. Try different positions with your arms but never have them wide. Don't expect this position to be easy to hold – it will take a lot of practice just to maintain it for several seconds. The next step is to start turning from this position. Never start a manoeuvre until at least ten seconds after leaving the plane, as you won't have gained enough air speed to get going. Turns are made as usual, by tilting the body top slightly and using your arms. Start by lowering one arm into the airflow in the direction you want to go and bring the other hand over that way too, with elbow bent and palm cupped to catch the air and the back of the hand facing towards the way you want to

You will need to work at your 'small' position on the ground before trying it in the air.

turn. Either keep your legs in tight (this will take a lot of practice as the automatic reaction is to let them drift out) or relax them a little for the beginning of the turn and then bring them back in sharply as the turn takes. You will have to put in a lot of hard work before you develop a method of turning that suits your own particular style. There are two main methods of turning: one is the static method, where you use just your arms and the rest of your body remains tightly curled up, and the other is the pulsating method, where you use your whole body to help spin you round.

To start with, you will have to stop each manoeuvre before going into the next. Once you can do turns – if not very fast, at least under control – start doing loops.

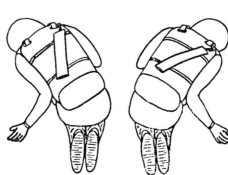

Fig. 5 The static method is where you turn using your arms only and keeping your legs tightly tucked up.

You may well have gone through your student days by throwing your head back as you go into the loop. But this should never be done on a style jump. Just as you should keep the body tight to make turns on a pivot, you need to keep tight to turn a backloop quickly. If you open your body out as you go over on a backloop it will have much further to turn before it finishes the loop. So keep your head down and your legs tucked up and just use your arms. Push them out straight and not too wide in front of you, with palms facing the earth. If the rest of the body is tight, that is all you need to do to flip over – the speed will surprise you!

Once you have got some sort of a basis to work from, the next step is the transition from one manoeuvre to another. The best way to stop a turn is by initiating a turn in the opposite direction. In style, you just hold this opposite position a little longer, and you will spin round the other way. Style jumps never include two consecutive turns in the same direction, so once you can do a fast turn and then stop it by quickly going into a turn in the opposite direction you are getting on well.

Turns to backloops are more difficult. Once you are three quarters of the way round the turn, you must start slowly bringing your hands up and out, so that as you spin to the end of your turn your arms plunge straight out in front of you to lift you into that backloop. This needs a lot of good timing and anticipation. The same anticipation is called for in the transition from loop to turn. As you go over the top of the loop your arms need to be coming in and dropping so that as you come up from the loop you immediately go into another tight turn. If you start the turn at the right moment the throw-forward from the loop will speed you up on your turn. If you do it too late you will find you have done another half backloop before you start to turn, wasting a lot of time and probably losing control of the series. Control and anticipation are two of the key words for style. When you start going faster you will start making errors – not completing a turn or going on round past the heading (the way you were facing when you started) before starting to go the other way. All such errors mean penalties on your final time, so from the start always try to be aware of your heading.

A lot of style jumpers like to turn their series facing the pit, but any building, field, runway, or anything that is easily visible will do for you to start turning over. When you have done a lot of style you should be able to turn a set without looking at your heading, but it takes a while before you get to that stage. Once you can turn a whole set in 9 or 10 seconds you will have developed a basic style, and then you will need to analyse every movement to see where you are losing time and how you can speed up your set. This is where a video unit can save you lots of work, as it films you close up in the air and you can watch yourself over and over when you are back on the ground, identifying exactly where you are going wrong or where you could improve. Many jumpers go into a steep dive once they are out of the plane. They will dive for perhaps 12 or 15 seconds, gaining as much speed as possible before instantly going into their first rapid turn.

Style in Competition Work

In competition the style manoeuvres are drawn from the following:

Left set	left turn, right turn, loop, left turn, right turn, loop.
Right set	right turn, left turn, loop, right turn, left turn, loop.
Left cross	left turn, right turn, loop, right turn, left turn, loop.
Right cross	right turn, left turn, loop, left turn, right turn, loop.

If there are more than four rounds, then the additional rounds are drawn from the above. Jumping height is from 1800–2000 m (5900–6600 ft) which gives between 22 and 27 seconds' working time. You are timed from the moment you start your first turn to the moment you come up through the horizontal degree on your last loop. You are given penalty points in the form of half a second or a second or even more for undershooting turns, losing heading on the loops, or for any other deviation on any of the manoeuvres. There is a maximum score for each series and you are automatically given this if you do a wrong manoeuvre or any additional manoeuvre on the jump.

Relative Work

Relative work is fantastic fun. It isn't so many years ago that a star of perhaps eight or ten jumpers linked together in the air was quite an achievement. Today there are competitions where teams of sixteen

Relative work is always fun.

Every relative jump must be practised carefully on the ground first.

jumpers link together, split up and come together again in different groups, and many jumpers take part in sixteen-, twenty-, even thirty- and forty-man stars and other formations. But as with any other aspect of this sport, success demands hard work and constant practice, and also quite a lot of good weather with clear skies so that you can get enough height. Whatever the jump – from a basic three- or four-man link to an eight- or sixteen-man sequential jump which includes several different formations – the whole jump *must* be practised on the ground. These rehearsals are paramount if you are going to have a successful jump. Start the practice with the whole team in the plane on the ground, fully kitted up, and go through all the movements and formations.

Exits have to be as near simultaneous as possible to ensure the minimum distance between the jumpers as they leave the plane. The easiest method of ensuring that everybody is ready to leave at the same time is the counting method. Most groups yell *three, two, one, go* and on the word *go* they all push out of the door together, staying as close as possible as they start making their formations in freefall. As you progress into complicated formations, you will not only have slot numbers (for example, you may be third or fourth man to close in on the base group) but also slot positions, i.e. you approach the base group from one specific side and dock (fly into the group) between two named members of the group. So this all has to be practised on the ground – the last thing you want to do is waste valuable air time wondering where you are meant to be going!

Quick exits are imperative on relative jumps so that there is minimal separation between jumpers.

'Sequential' is the term applied to a group making different formations on the same jump. From a basic round star you can split into a doughnut, a line, or any other of the many recognized formations. Once you are into sequential work, it is vital that you practise docking backwards and sideways as well as using the normal head-forward approach, because you will need to enter certain formations side or feet first. A four-man in/out, for instance, is built by two jumpers flying in slightly sideways and turning their legs to a base man before the fourth jumper closes the slot. It is always better to fly into a formation in the correct position for the manoeuvre than to go in head first and then change grip and work your way round to the right position.

Once you have docked, good grips are vital. Flying a formation properly is probably more difficult than building it, and the larger it is the more unwieldy it becomes. The best way is for everyone to maintain his own flying momentum in his slot, not relying on his grip to keep him in place. This releases the pressure on the grips and also exerts minimal pressure on the formation. A good way to practise this is on 'no contact' jumps, where you fly down to your slot, but instead of actually linking and taking hold of someone's jumpsuit you stay a few inches away and try to keep in the right position.

As you progress to advanced sequential work, the intermediate steps from one formation to another sometimes have to be flown to a precise pattern as well. Perhaps a sixteen-man splits into four lots of four men, and each of the four groups has to fly as a group into the new formation. This isn't as difficult as it sounds, but the main thing is to make sure your group stays close to the other groups. If you slide away it takes quite a bit of flying to get your group across to the other groups again. The same applies for manoeuvres where everyone breaks grip before reforming. So one important rule is to stay as close together as possible. It is easier to do relative work in wide baggy jumpsuits. With a whole team wearing very loose suits, resistance to the airflow is greater, which means they can fly and dock more steadily.

Fig. 6 Four-person formations

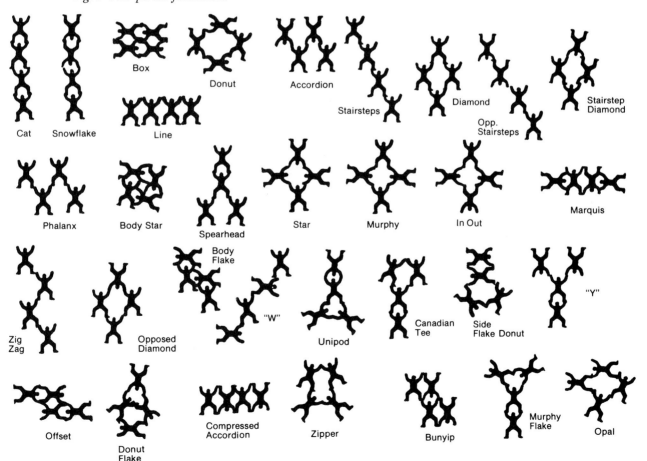

When jumping in big groups, it is vital to separate before opening your parachutes. The bigger the group, the higher you will all have to break up so that you have enough time to track away from each other before opening the chute. When you are working hard in sequential it is impossible to keep looking at your altimeter. Instead, one particular jumper is nominated to watch the height and give a definite wave-off when it is time to break. The best way to progress in relative work is to get together with a group of friends and jump together for a while, so that you get to know how everyone flies and can work on problems together.

Competition in Relative Work

Relative competitions are held at club, regional and national levels, and there are also several big international meets every year. Rules vary from meet to meet, from ten- and twenty-man speed stars (i.e. you are marked on the time taken to make the formation) to the popular four- and eight-man sequential contests. Here rounds usually alternate between set sequences and random sequences. A set sequence means the jumpers have to make several different formations in the air, one after the other, and on the intermediate steps between the formations the jumpers will be required to fly together in specific groups. In random rounds there has to be complete separation of the jumpers between the formations.

These competitions can be scored in several ways, but usually there is a set of perhaps five manoeuvres, and the team scores for every formation completed. When they have completed all five formations they start again and go on working until their time has run out. Omission of a formation, incorrect completion of a formation, incorrect transition manoeuvre or incorrect formation according to the sequence will stop the scoring. Exit altitudes vary, but most contests stipulate 3250 m (11000 ft) for eight-man events and 2750 m (9000 ft) for four-man events.

Canopy Relative Work

Canopy relative work involves linking up with another jumper under an opened square parachute, and this should only be attempted when you are familiar with your parachute and how it flies. Always start by jumping with someone who has done a lot of canopy relative work before, and don't immediately try for a link-up. Instead, open

Flying in groups forms part of international relative competition.

the parachutes higher than normal to give yourselves more time, and just manoeuvre the canopies close together without actually touching. This alone will be more difficult than it sounds, as your rate of descent and forward speed can vary so much. Try to keep close and take note of the difference in the flights of the two parachutes, so that you can adjust your own flying to keep alongside the other parachute. Don't come up on the same level directly behind another square parachute as you will get into its backwash, and your canopy could become radically unstable.

Before you take off for an attempted hook-up, you must decide who is going to be the aggressor (the one who does the linking up) and who is going to be the target (the low man). To begin with, let the experienced jumper be the aggressor. Once the parachutes are open, the target man must be below – if you both open at the same height the easiest way for the target man to lose height is by pulling down on the front risers of his parachute. Ideally the two parachutes should start by flying facing the same way but with the aggressor a little higher and off to one side. The low man or target should be flying on 50 to 60 per cent brakes so that the high man can come forward or go back as necessary. The target jumper should now make a *very slow* turn right or left towards the aggressor. This allows the two parachutes to meet up at equal speeds and similar rates of descent, and is based on the 'lead pursuit curve'. Pilots found out years ago that this technique was the best way to rendezvous two aero-

planes, and the same theory stands for flying ram-air parachutes. The aggressor must make very slow movements, and should approach the target parachute at a very steady rate.

The usual way to link is for the aggressor to make his way to the side of the target parachute, and then line his parachute up so that both canopies are flying forward and the aggressor is flying alongside the parachute of the target jumper. Then he manoeuvres close enough until he can reach out and take a grip of the top front edge of the parachute. *Never* grip any part of the target parachute other than the top leading edge of the upper surface. To take hold of stabilizers, the tail, suspension lines or any other part can cause instability and even canopy collapse, which means a face full of flapping nylon for the aggressor, no support in the air for the target man, and possible disaster for both jumpers. Also never fly across the top of the other parachute – if your foot gets caught up in the bridle cord or pilot chute both of you may have a problem.

Once you have a grip, ideally on the top front seam with the fingers over the edge of the material, trim your parachute with the other hand until it is flying smoothly. If it is oscillating badly and you cannot stop it with one hand, let go and get settled before making another approach. Once you are flying together, let go the other toggle and move your other hand down to take a firm grip of the parachute. Spread your hands out so they are gripping firmly behind you, and slowly edge your way, cell by cell, until you are right in the middle of the target parachute. Then pull the top of the leading edge you are gripping up behind your back until you can slip your feet into one of the centre cells. Turn your toes out and tuck them into the material on the walls of the cell, though don't push out too much with your feet. Then gently stand up, letting go of the parachute, and take hold of the toggles on your own parachute again. And there you have it. The top jumper is always in control of both parachutes – the lower jumper won't be able to steer at all.

Once you want to separate, just let go and fly off to the side. Never flare off backwards, as you will sink back into the backwash created by the lower canopy. When two jumpers are flying linked up, a third jumper can attempt to get on the top parachute by the same method, and then a fourth, and so on. But with several jumpers linked you'll find the stack tends to fly at an angle with the top canopy well forward and the lowest parachute well back, and this can be very difficult to hold.

(facing) *Canopy relative work requires a tremendous amount of skill.*

Chapter 8

BUYING THE RIGHT EQUIPMENT

Before you purchase any piece of equipment, spend a little time checking whether it really is exactly what you want. Today there is a tremendous variety of shapes, sizes and colours available in student and advanced equipment, and although some things look similar they don't always do the same job. Students don't need to splash out on a lot of new equipment. While it is nice to have a parachute in the colour of your choice and a backpack and harness in contrasting colours, if you progress normally you will soon be swapping this gear for more advanced equipment. Most clubs have notice-boards, so see what student equipment is available second-hand and get an instructor to check it over before you purchase. Jumpsuits, boots, helmet and goggles, altimeter and reserve parachute are basics that a student jumper can invest in because they should last for as long as he needs them.

Advanced equipment varies tremendously. New ideas are constantly coming onto the market, only to be followed by something even newer a few months later. Make sure you know what you want, and if you are ever in doubt about the workings of a new idea consult an expert in that line before you buy.

Jumpsuits

Colours and patterns vary, but jumpsuits usually come big, baggy and flared with wide arms and legs for relative workers, and tight, stretchy and fitted for style jumpers. Most jumpers who enjoy each aspect of the sport will need both. Some jumpers prefer to jump in tracksuits or other suitable clothing of their own choice.

Gloves

Gloves can be reasonably thick to protect the fingers from cold on icy winter days and to grab more air for good freefall manoeuvrability, but they must not be so thick that they interfere with movement, especially in an emergency when the main parachute has to be released.

Harness

This can be bought made to measure and with minimal adjustment, or be fully adjustable so that it fits anyone. While made-to-measure harnesses should always be comfortable, they can be a problem to sell second-hand as you must either find someone exactly your size or have the harness altered.

Cut-away systems

Many new systems are now in use to attach the risers and parachute to the harness and yet facilitate quick and safe ejection of the main parachute in emergencies. They range between the all-metal two-shots that require two separate movements to release them and the modern fabric and metal R2 and R3 systems that release instantly when you pull down a fabric or plastic tab. Whichever type you choose, make sure you completely understand how and why it works before you install it on your equipment.

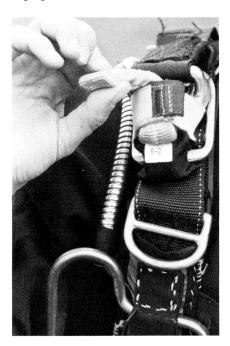

Many different types of cut-away systems are now in use, including the popular R2 system.

Backpacks and reserve containers
There are two main systems: the conventional system, in which the
back container holds the main parachute and the reserve is worn on
the front; and a system used only by advanced jumpers called the
piggy-back or hog-back system, where the reserve is worn on the

There are two main types of container: the conventional system (above) *where the reserve
pack is worn separately on the front; and the piggyback* (below), *where the reserve is
incorporated with the main pack and worn on the back.*

back above the main parachute. It is really just a question of what you can work best in, though generally relative jumpers prefer the piggy-back system because there is less air resistance to fast horizontal movement.

Ripcords and throwaways
While the ripcord system has been the traditional method of opening the parachute for many years, new ideas are now coming onto the market. The throwaway system does away with the ripcord and pilot chute spring. It is a very popular alternative and should eliminate pilot chute hesitations.

Main parachutes
With advanced round parachutes your choice will again depend very much on what you are doing. For accuracy work the UT 15 and Papillon parachutes are probably the most popular, with their fast stable turns and good braking systems, but many other equally good designs are available. It is best to try out a few parachutes, borrowing them from friends and clubs, before making a final decision.

Square ram-air parachutes vary in size and shape too, some being more unstable than others, some with faster forward speeds, lower descent rates and so on. The strato-star parachute was the first really popular square parachute. The strato-clouds and 252s came out a little later, and because of their steady flight in deep brakes were pounced on by accuracy workers. The newer strato-flyers became a favourite with relative workers because of their lightness and compactness. Many new ideas and designs are now on the drawing-boards, but to continue to enjoy your jumping as well as safeguard your investment it is not a bad idea to let a new type of parachute prove itself before you buy.

Reserve parachutes
Students use basic round unsteerable reserves, but once you are an experienced jumper it is up to you to choose a reserve that you are happy with and that will fit into the reserve pack on your equipment. Steerable reserves are available, which are a good idea in case you are blown onto obstacles, and also can be turned into the wind and give a softer landing.

Chapter 9

PACKING

Right from the start, every jumper is taught to pack his or her own rig. It is not a difficult thing to do once you are familiar with a parachute, and it has to be learnt if you want to stay in the sport, as no one will have the time continually to pack for you. At first your packing will be carefully supervised by a qualified packer, but once you have earned your packing certificates you will be on your own.

Round Parachutes

Whether these are advanced parachutes with several modifications or basic double-ls, the theory is the same. The parachute must be laid out flat with the apex at one end and the canopy and lines stretched down to the risers and harness at the other. The lines and the nylon material of the canopy must be checked to see that they are clear of any entanglements. The lines should lie together down the centre, and the canopy must be pulled out at each side. You will find the parachute will naturally fall into two halves, the right-hand side being attached to the lines from the right risers, the left-hand side being attached to the lines from the left risers. Every nylon gore between the lines must now be carefully pulled out and straightened, starting from the lowest gore nearest the table or the ground and ending with the gore on the top. Once all the lines are absolutely straight and the fabric pulled neatly out, with each gore folded on top of the next, then you should be able to look up the centre inside

You are always taught to pack for yourself, right from the beginning.

the parachute and check it is clear. This is where the air will rush into on opening. The next step depends on the type of system you are using. Either a long protective sleeve is pulled down over the para-chute, or the parachute is folded carefully into an inner bag. Once the parachute is packed away in a sleeve or inner bag, then the lines are stowed in elastic bands attached to the sleeve or bag. This keeps them neat and stops them from becoming entangled, but lets them pull out easily on opening. Then the sleeve or bag is put in the outer container, the pilot-chute is compressed and put in on top, and the pack is shut.

Square Parachutes

The packing principle is the same with squares. Once the jump is over, the canopy must be laid down flat on one side, with the lines stretched out straight to the harness at the other end. Once the lines are straight,

89

then the fabric of the parachute must be pulled out and neatened. With most square parachutes the best way is to pull out the top seams, which will ensure all the cells are tidy underneath. Because of their design square parachutes can open very quickly, and this can hurt a jumper if he goes instantly from freefall into a slow descent under the parachute. Therefore various devices have been fitted to square parachutes to slow down the opening sequence and arrest the speed of the jumper gently. The most common is the slider system – a small nylon square with metal eyelets in each corner that holds the parachute lines together and then slowly slides down the lines. This slider has to be pulled back up to the top of the lines on packing, or if another method is in use then this must be re-applied. The parachute can be folded, one section on top of another, or rolled from each end into the middle, depending again on what sort of slowing device is being used. The lines are stowed in rubber bands, or in some cases coiled freely in the bottom of the container. Then the parachute is put into the backpack, the pilot chute is compressed and put on top, and the pack is shut.

Packing shouldn't take much more than twenty minutes – some jumpers can do it in half the time. But speed isn't the main thing. Rushed and untidy canopy packing can cause not only malfunctions but also burn holes and cause other damage to the parachute. Parachutes cost a lot of money, so it makes sense to pack carefully.

Appendix A

Glossary

Altimeter   The instrument which indicates a jumper's altitude above ground.

Apex   The top of a round parachute.

Canopy   The parachute.

Capewell   A quick-release system to separate harness from parachute.

Clear and pull   To open a parachute immediately after leaving the aeroplane.

Cut-away   The intentional releasing of the main parachute in an emergency.

Deployment   The unfolding and opening of the parachute.

Dummy ripcord pull   The simulated pulling of a ripcord (by a student) on an automatically opened parachute.

DZ   The dropping zone or landing area.

Freefall   The time spent in the air after leaving the plane but before opening the parachute.

Frog   A relaxed freefall position.

Holding   Facing into the wind under the parachute to reduce drift.

Jumpmaster   The senior parachutist in charge of a plane full of jumpers.

Malfunction   An improper opening of the parachute.

Pilot chute   A small parachute which is released into the air first to pull out the main parachute.

PLF   Parachute landing fall.

Relative work   The art of linking up with one, two or more parachutists in freefall.

Ripcord   The handle and cable which are pulled to open the backpack.

Risers   The webbing that attaches the harness to the lines of the parachute.

Spotting   Guiding the plane to the right exit point so that the parachutists leave the plane in the right place.

Stable spread   The arched and stretched position used by students.

Static line   The length of webbing attached to the aircraft and parachute used for automatic openings.

Style   A series of six specific turns and backloops performed in freefall.

Terminal velocity   The greatest speed a body will reach in freefall.

WDI   The length of crêpe paper thrown from the aircraft to determine wind speed and direction.

Appendix B

System of Parachutist Classification

Category 1   Has been passed out on basic ground training (minimum 6 hours) and is ready for first static-line descent.

Category 2   a) Has performed a minimum of three absolutely stable observed static-line descents in the full spread position, counting throughout.

b) Has completed a total of 13 hours of ground training in accordance with the minimum ground training programme.

Category 3   Has performed a minimum of three successful and consecutive observed static-line descents with dummy ripcord, counting throughout.

Category 4 (5 seconds)

a) Has performed a minimum of five stable 5-second delayed openings.

b) Has remained stable throughout opening on each descent.

c) Has looked at ripcord handle before and during the 'reach and pull'.

d) Has achieved reasonable canopy handling.

Category 5 (10 seconds)

a) Has performed a minimum of five stable 10-second delayed openings, counting throughout.

b) Has learned to maintain heading during exit and in freefall.

Category 6 (15 seconds)

a) Has performed a minimum of five stable 15-second delayed openings in the following sequence:
i) two flat stable descents, counting throughout.
ii) after instruction in the use of instruments, three flat stable descents, using instruments but continuing to count throughout.

b) After successful completion of (a) has demonstrated his ability to perform 360° turns in each direction, stopping on the aircraft heading.

Category 7 (20 seconds)

a) Has performed a minimum of five stable 20-second delayed openings.

b) Has demonstrated his ability to recover from an unstable position on leaving the aircraft.

c) Has been introduced to spotting.

Category 8 (30 seconds)

a) Has landed within 50 m (50 yards) of centre of target on a minimum of three 30-second delayed-opening descents.

b) Has learned to track and to turn in a track.

c) Has been cleared for self-spotting up to 2100 m (7000 ft).

On completion of category 8, the student may be recommended for an FAI C certificate by his instructor and introduced to a para-commander or similar type of high-performance canopy.

Category 9   a) Has demonstrated to an instructor in freefall that he is fully in control of his movements, is aware of other parachutists around him and is capable of taking avoiding action.

b) Has demonstrated his ability to perform aerial manoeuvres, for example loops and rolls.

c) Has been introduced to relative parachuting.

Category 10   a) Has been cleared for unsupervised relative work, having successfully demonstrated the following: pin, backloop, pin with a category 10 jumper approved by the club's chief instructor, on a single jump.

b) Has closed third on two occasions.

c) Has been cleared for self-spotted descents up to 3500 m (12000 ft).

Appendix C

FAI Certificates

A certificate	Category 3 and 10 jumps.
B certificate	Category 5 and 25 jumps to include 10 jumps landing within 50 m (150 ft) of the target.
C certificate	Category 8 and 50 jumps to include 20 jumps landing within 20 m (60 ft) of the target.
D certificate	Category 10 and 200 freefall jumps to include 20 jumps landing within 15 m (45 ft) of the target.

Appendix D

Useful Addresses

Associations

The British Parachute Association,
Kimberly House,
47 Vaughan Way,
Leicester LE1 4SG

Tel. Leicester 59778/59635

Scottish Sport Parachuting Association,
99 West Torbain,
Kirkcaldy,
Fife

Tel. Kirkcaldy 200042

British Collegiate Parachute Association,
The Spread Eagle,
Broad Lane,
Wednesfield,
Wolverhampton

Army Parachute Association,
JSPC Airfield Camp,
Netheravon,
Wiltshire

RAF Sport Parachute Association,
RAF Brize Norton,
Oxon

Royal Navy and Royal Marines Sport
Parachute Association,
Commando Training Centre RM,
Lympstone,
Exmouth,
Devon EX8 5AR

The Skydiving Club,
15 Upper Beaumont Drive,
Ballintemple,
Cork,
Eire

United States Parachute Association,
806 Fifteenth Street NW,
Suite 444
Washington DC 20005
USA

Canadian Sport Parachute Association,
National Sport and Recreation Centre,
333 River Road,
Vanier City,
Ontario KIL 8B9,
Canada

Parachute Committee,
Aero Club of South Africa,
PO Box 2312,
Johannesburg 2000,
Republic of South Africa

Australian Parachute Federation,
PO Box 21,
Doveton,
Victoria 3177,
Australia

New Zealand Parachute Club,
4 Delange St,
Christchurch 4,
New Zealand

Clubs

The British Parachute Association can supply a full list of the thirty-five clubs currently operating in Britain. The majority are open at weekends only, but full-time parachute centres include:

Peterborough Parachute Centre,
Sibson Airfield,
Wansford,
Peterborough

Tel. Elton 490

Hereford Parachute Club Ltd,
Shobdon Aerodrome,
Leominster,
Hereford

Tel. Kingsland 551

RSA Parachute Club,
Thruxton Aerodrome,
Andover,
Hants

Tel. Weyhill 2124

Eagle Sport Parachute Centre,
Ashford Airport,
Lympne,
Kent

Tel. Hythe 60816

The Sport Parachute Club,
Bridlington Aerodrome,
Bridlington,
Yorkshire

Bridlington 77367

East Coast Parachute Centre,
Ipswich Airport,
Ipswich,
Suffolk

Tel: 0473 70111 ext 10